Errors
in the
Script

For Martha,
It's really a pleasure
to meet you. Keep fighting
the good fight with the grass.

Best Wishes,
Greg

Errors in the Script

poems

Greg Williamson

Greg Williamson

Sewanee, 2006

SEWANEE WRITERS' SERIES / THE OVERLOOK PRESS

SEWANEE WRITERS' SERIES/THE OVERLOOK PRESS
First published in the United States in 2001 by
The Overlook Press, Peter Mayer Publishers, Inc.
Woodstock & New York

Woodstock:
One Overlook Drive / Woodstock, NY 12498
www.overlookpress.com
[for individual orders, bulk and special sales]

New York:
386 West Broadway / New York, NY 10012

ACKNOWLEDGMENTS

Crab Orchard Review: "Holiday Mall with LONG FENCE"; "Plumber in Crawl
Space under New York City Skyline"; *The Formalist:* "Kites at the Washington
Monument"; "New Year's: A Short Pantoum"; *Kenyon Review:* "Binocular
Diplopia"; *The New Young American Poets: An Anthology:* "Appalachian Trees
Encircled by Police Tape"; *New England Review:* "Bodies of Water"; *Paris
Review:* "Self-Portrait of the Artist in a Mirror with Ghost"; "Half Border
Collie, Half Black Strip"; *Pivot:* "Origami"; *Pleiades:* "Group Photo with Winter
Trees"; *Poetry:* "Medical School Skeleton with Dominoes Pizza Man"; "Profiles:
Anne Dancing with Skeleton"; *Raritan:* "On or about His Birthday"; *River Styx:*
"Girl on Bicycle with American Kestrel"; "Photo Album with Visiting Couple
Misfolding Afghan"; *Sewanee Theological Review:* "Visiting Couple Kissing and
Halved Onion"; *Southwest Review:* "Nervous Systems"; "Errors in the Script";
Story: "The Top Priority"; *Sundog:* "Portrait of the Artist's Feet with High Top
Mtn."; "View of a Neighborhood in West Nashville with UFO"; *Yale Review:*
"The Dark Days"; "Three-Sided, One-Way Mirror"

Library of Congress Cataloging-in-Publication Data

Williamson, Greg.
Errors in the Script.
p. cm.
(Sewanee writer's series)
I. Title II. Series.
PS3573.I456273 E77 2001   811'.54—dc21   00-051512

Book design and type formatting by Bernard Schleifer
Manufactured in the United States of America
First Edition
1 3 5 7 9 8 6 4 2
ISBN 1-58567-117-7

for Karen

Contents

III.

. . . and a table of green fields.

—*Henry V*, III.iii.15

I.

Origami

The kids are good at this. Their nimble fingers
Double and fold and double fold the pages,
Making mimetic icons for all ages.
The floor of the school is littered with dead ringers:

Songbirds that really flap their wings, rare cranes,
Bleached bonsai trees, pale ghouls, two kinds of hats,
Dwarf stars, white roses, Persian copycats,
Small packet boats, whole fleets of flyable planes.

Some of the girls, some of the older ones,
Make effigies of boys and . . . "Goodness sakes!"
They ask what I can make. "I make mistakes."
"No really, Mr. Greg!" They don't like puns.

I tear out a page and say, "I've made a bed."
They frown at me. I'll have to lie on it.
"See, it's a sheet." But they're not buying it,
And seem to imply ("you crazy!") it's all in my head.

I head for home, where even more white lies
Take shape. The page is a window filled with frost,
An unformed thought, a thought I had, but lost.
The page is the sclera of someone rolling his eyes

As it becomes (you'll recognize the trick)
Tomorrow morning, laundry on the line,
The South Pole, circa 1929,
The mainsail of the *Pequod*, Moby Dick,

The desert sand, the shore, the arctic waste
Of untold tales, where hero and author together
Must turn, out of the silence, into the whether-
Or-not-they-find-the-grail. Not to your taste?

The page is a flag of surrender. I surrender—
To the rustle of programs before a serious talk,
The sound of seashells, seas, the taste of chalk,
The ghost of snow, the ghost of the sky in December,

And frozen surfaces of ponds, which hide
Some frigid stirring, something. (What have I done?)
It's the napkin at a table set for one,
The shade drawn in a room where someone died.

The pages keep on turning. They assume
More shapes than I can put my finger on,
A wall of silence, curtains, doors, false dawn,
The stared-at ceiling of my rented room.

"You crazy, Mr. Greg." The voices call.
The sheet on the unmade bed is gone awry.
I sit at my little desk in mid-July
Throwing snowballs at the Sheetrock wall.

Kites at the Washington Monument

What's up, today, with our lovers?

W. D. SNODGRASS

At fingertip control
　These state-of-the-art stunt kites
Chandelle, wingover, and roll
　To dive from conspicuous heights,

Whatever the pilots will,
　While the wowed audience follows
As the kites come in for the kill
　And slice up the air like swallows.

But look, across the park
　Someone has put together—
What is it? It looks like a lark
　Tossed up into the weather.

It's homemade out of paper
　That tumbles and bobs like a moth
On another meaningless caper.
　Why, it's a bit of froth

Spun on a blue lake,
　A name or a wrinkled note
Dropped into the wake
　Of an ocean-going boat.

15

But still it pulls itself higher
   As he would pull it back.
The line goes tight as wire,
   Or sags, falling, and goes slack,

And while the audience claps
   At the aerobatic buzz,
It flutters, quiets, then it snaps.
   But that's about all it does.

Flying its tail of rags
   Above these broken lands,
It's one of those white flags
   For things that are out of our hands,

The hoisted colors of
   Attenuated hope,
The handkerchief of a love
   That's come to the end of its rope.

When the line breaks, the string
   Floats to the ground in the wind.
He stands there watching the thing
   Still holding up his end

As the kite heads into the sky
   Like a sail leaving a slip.
The rags wave goodbye.
   They're scarves at the back of a ship.

On or about His Birthday

Party of one: the shower, the cake of soap,
The buttery toast to which he raised his cup
Of tea. Having discarded the envelope
Of sugar and perused the horoscope,
     "Big deal at work turns up,"

And having lit the citronella candle
And wandered (lonely as a cloud) to check
The Crimson Jack tomato vines that dandle
Emerald solitaires, he loosens a sandal
     And sits, all hands on deck.

If the sun's a gift, rising above the gable,
If begonias in the window bloom like bows,
If liriope turns to ribbon, it's a fable
And he's the intrusive speaker. At the table
     He sets the cards in rows,

And instantly the catalpa's full of hearts;
Exclusive clubs of finch and chickadee
Shuffle around the feeder, playing their parts
In the running commentary, which imparts:
     Black two on red three.

The grass is wet with diamonds, and the spade
In the ground he calls a spade. The serpentine
Hose is a six on which a pothook's played
By the one-eyed jack, who never learned a trade.
      Red eight on black nine.

Big deal at work. If things turned up they'd find
The clouds of icing turn to floating cakes
Of French vanilla, layered and refined.
What turns up next, what comes to the floating mind,
      Is he and the clouds are fakes.

They might be sawdust clouds of cabinetwork,
Cities of smog, exhaust, the thick cascade
Of refinery smoke, lobbies where bankers smirk.
Black seven on red eight. Big deal at work.
      He never learned a trade.

And soon enough the sun will set. The vines
Will drop their fruit. The bows will fall. The fall
Will see the birds depart, as he cosigns
Another loan, in some nonce place. The signs
      Are there. If you can call

It work, he sees how the pattering mind will cope
With what the heart is feeling, like reading a cup
Of tea leaves, cloud banks, cards, the horoscope.
He shuffles the deck. He'll play his cards and hope
      Whatever he needs turns up.

The Top Priority

Granted I am a malcontent, a geek,
Whose people skills and interfacing technique
Are, let's say, challenged; granted I maintain
A kennel of pet peeves, and yet this reign
Of fashion needs a simple boy to focus
On our nude king, the cheeky hocus-pocus
Of base, Orwellian duplicitese:
Free gifts, true facts, and top priorities.

At JFK the ticket engineer
Invites us to pre-board. I down my beer
Then stash the paperback and check my fly.
That isn't what she means. I don't know why.
She says to us, who clearly aren't on board,
"Those who have not pre-boarded now may board."
And when we land in the weather event called rain,
Do we de-board? It turns out we de-plane.
I've left, egressed, dismounted, not remained;
But the hitch de-planing is, we never planed.

Granted I am a grump, a grouch, a crank,
But when the recipe for braised lamb shank
Au dik-dik says, "Preheat the oven to,"
If it said, "Heat the oven," what would you do?
If grocery stores supply a pre-sliced roll,
And sliced is sliced, pre-sliced is what? Well, whole.

If the sales clerk suggests a pre-made bow,
You think that he means ribbon. Does he? No.
When Deal Dan says, "Not 'used,' 'pre-*owned*' Crown Vic,"
You ask him, "Did she use it?" He says, "Dick."
If soup is ready-to-eat, what soup is not?
The kind that's rice, a chicken, and a pot.
And this kind, too, because there is no pan,
No bowl, no spoon, it's cold, it's in a can.
And why not offer ready-to-fish-with hooks,
Or ready-to-read, pre-bound, pre-written books?

We call things "literal" when figurative:
"I literally died." And yet you live.
We float a metaphor until it fails:
"The steam was taken out of the president's sails."
We drown correctness in polluted waters:
"Woman admits to allegedly killing her daughters."
We dress plain subjects up in regal guise:
To talk is "to share"; to plan, "prioritize";
And the big business, when its growing ceases,
"Rightsizes," when, more rightly, it decreases.
We form tautologies defying sense,
As with, say, "previous experience,"
"Past history," or when the poet wrote,
"Then I can truly forgive her." By a vote
The class refused to find the phrase unruly.
Later I forgave them, but not truly,

And add my errors to the list, of course.
I have misspoken, riding my high horse,
But hope I'm truly forgiven every lie.
And so, you know, like, basically, when I die,
Pre-dig my grave six feet to hide the coffin,
Brainstorm and dialogue about me often,

And I'll de-body to join the win-win group
For pre-cooked ham and ready-to-eat soup,
Completely free gifts, no extra charge to me,
And walk with God, the Top Priority.

Bodies of Water

Yes, but the body is made of water. That's
      A fact. It freezes with fear
And boils with rage because it has its states.
      It blows off steam. It swells with pride.
        It sweats like a pipe,
        But it is water.

Genetic pool, swamp of desires, its heart
      Melts at a beautiful face;
Turned to a puddle, it stands in the street and admires.
      The body runs hot and cold and down
        In soaked beds,
        Seeking its level.

There have been souls who drowned in pity, drowned
      In sorrow. Just last week
There was a glimmer of something out on the surface,
      Then it went under. When divers went in
        They found gold teeth
        And hundreds of miles of water.

Nervous Systems

And the crack in the tea-cup opens
A lane to the land of the dead.

W. H. AUDEN

Not many trees survive our satellite
Communities. But here by a quiet house
And fanned by warm midmorning breeze, daylight
Flares in a living ash, where dark birds light
On ramifying, migratory routes.
And then this warning flashes on the light
Meter: Inside the house a pilot light
Is always burning in the oven's eyes,
And the low roof is pulled down over the eyes
Like a hat, and underneath the morning's leit-
Motif networks of subterranean lines
Run like the nervous system, or bloodlines,

Or fractures spreading from tectonic lines
Of fault. From distant coasts, heavy and light
Petroleum is piped across state lines,
And gas, electric, oil, and water lines
Convey their vital humors to the house.
The greatest threat to all these bottom lines
Remains the operator who declines
To call for information about their routes
But sinks the backhoe's teeth among the roots.
An accident explodes in the headlines,
Rattling the suburb's glassy eyes,
Or seeps into the ground beneath our eyes,

Avoiding, for a time, the public's eyes.
The leak spreads like reticulating lines
Of thought, which thinks of crow's-feet at the eyes,
Or secret guilt dilating in your eyes,
Something you hope is never brought to light,
Or mysteries behind your neighbor's eyes,
Or else the casual way we shut our eyes
To dark forebodings lurking in the house-
Hold phrase, our faults that may bring down the house.
There's a screw loose, blown fuse, fire in the eyes,
Frayed nerves, live wires. Like words out of taproots,
The pipes break off on long, anfractuous routes.

Bearing in mind the origin of "routes"
Is *rumpere*, "to rupture," cast your eyes
On the thriving industry of thrift, which roots
In the cracked sidewalks, cracking with the roots.
There's something going on between the lines,
Below our feet, baring along their routes
Whatever's buried with the bitter roots.
Across the seeded lawn, by a floodlight,
A sassafras is spreading toward the light,
But it has "stone" and "breaker" in its roots.
It's growing at the corner of the house,
Derived from *hydan*, "to hide," which gives us "house."

Thus, rarely do we see an open house.
Like Huntington's stalking in genetic roots—
Who can be sure what's growing up in-house,
In living rooms, in broken homes? They house,
Perhaps, deft infidelities, black eyes,
Crude violence to the children playing house.
The oven's eyes are burning in the house.
And you can almost hear, in the phone lines,
The hubbub that entreats, retracts, maligns.

A work truck sidles up beside the house.
Two men in hats and uniforms alight.
They have a pickaxe and a trouble light.

The underground is booming. Traveling light,
The pipelines work their way from house to house,
Operating among our darkest roots,
Like nervous systems tingling behind the eyes,
Conveying a threat, or something, along those lines.

The Dark Days

I. THE COLD WAR

We should have seen it coming back
In June: seeds of unrest, the troubled fiefdoms,
The snipers cloaked in blackjack oaks or sweet gums
    To launch an unprovoked attack

    On us with mace or Minié ball,
The ministers who joked about the sage,
The sage that withered up. In our bronze age
    We missed the heralds of a fall—

    The mounting shades, the Lilliputian
Insurrections waged by night—until
It dawned on us one morning with a chill:
    My God, another revolution.

    The trees ran up new banners, then
In bursts of color on a bombing run
Dropped propaganda leaflets. They had won.
    "Give up," we read. "You'll never win."

    In hindsight there's no mystery:
Too many palace coos, august parades,
Those slow mimosa Sundays, marmalades.
    Plus, we were young. That's history.

We should have seen it coming. Now
The slow smoke coils around the weathercocks,
All pointing north. We have set back our clocks,
    As if we could revive somehow

    Our flagging, fagged esprit de corps.
The parties are over. In personal retreats
The citizens observe the empty streets
    And the dark days of the cold war.

II. S.A.D.

We should have seen it coming? Back
In June, we're told, while sweets came to the suite,
The green, spring-loaded days were packing heat,
    And, even then, insomniac

Dark forces lurked in ambuscades;
Shadows were hatching cemetery plots;
And rebel sympathizers took potshots
    With cherry bombs and rusty blades,

Till one late dawn the songbirds peeled
Away. We woke to catapulting worry:
Hannibal ad portas! With a flurry
    The world turned. Winter swept the field.

Well, that's poetic elocution,
The civil war of words, that martial art
Ascribing nature with our purple heart.
    For me, another institution.

The light died like a summer fad.
I should have seen it coming? Naturally.
The season turned, in simple terms, on me.
    I'm sated, saturated, sad.

Sometimes I change the rheostat,
But still the slow smoke coils around the clocks,
All caged in wire. We walk around in socks
    And hear dust falling in the flat

White walls we turn our faces toward.
The poems are over. In partitioned rooms
The residents observe the long slow brooms
    And the dark daze of the cold ward.

III. Conspectus against Anthropocentric Assumptions in Polemical Rhetoric

We should have seen it. Coming back
In June, the sun achieved its northernmost
Ecliptic point, the solstice, which we post
    Beforehand in the almanac

And on which day our region sees
The maximum of solar lumination.
Because the planet's axis of rotation
    By $23.5°$

Inclines from perpendicular
To the Earth's plane of orbit, seasons change
With variations in the photic range
    Of our G2, main-sequence star.

Cork-celled abscission layers grow
On petioles of leaves. As chlorophyll
Dehydrates, pigments such as xanthophyll
    And carotene begin to show.

Climatic shifts that coincide
With mass migrations can contribute to,
In humans, elevated rates of flu,
    Fatigue, despair, and suicide.

Still, these are biological,
Not indications of occult intent.
We are a protoplasmic accident.
    That is the simple truth. Let all

Of nature's signal flags be furled.
The mysteries are over. God's dead. Nor
Should one detect some latent metaphor
    In the dark days of the cold world.

IV. Revised Weather Bulletin

We should have seen it coming back.
In "June" we should have heard the vestiges
Of "Juno," goddess of both marriages
    And war, and seen today's snowpack

Foreshadowed in the virgin plain
Of someone's bridal gown, blizzards of rice,
The glazed and frosted wedding cake, and ice-
    Bound, listing bottles of champagne,

Portending future dissolution.
We should have seen it coming back because,
While seasons change with scientific laws,
    Cf. another attribution:

"All things are metaphors," the Sage
Of Weimar said. And I have evidence,
The inside dope, counterintelligence:
    Flybys of geese, the heavy-gauge

Entanglements of trees, the charge
Of winter storm troops, and the clicking Morse
Of sleet detail the occupation force
    Of nature, standing by and large

For warfare, silencings, and fear.
Now long shades muster in the empty streets,
All choked in ice. The light brigade retreats
    To foothills of the last frontier,

And gray coats move in undeterred.
The year is over. In the studio
I see the long-range forecast calls for snow
    And the dark days of the cold word.

II.

Double Exposures

I. CAMERA SHAKE WITH WIDE-ANGLE
FIELD OF SNOW

        Just got these photos back. Let's have a look.
Now what the—? Tell me it's not an overprint.
        I thought, you know, I'd stick 'em in a book,
But look at those warped trees, the aqua tint,
        "My Life in Pictures." Now I'm not so sure.
Its long horizon's tipping off the page.
        I mean, what *is* that red-eyed, furry blur?
Since "photos capture life," then by my gauge,
        It's either my own Henry Pussycat,
Turning upon the blue, inclining snow,
        Or Yeti. Hmm. You'd think I'd remember that.
The world's a whole lot weirder than we know.

II. Outdoor Wedding
with Large Clock

   Phooey. I guess I'm no photographer:
You'll notice the clock looming above
   The old-style wedding is *another* blur,
And reminiscent of an era of
   Tall black top hats and antebellum gowns,
Great opulence. The hands are baroque; the tower,
   At this remove across the ample downs,
Almost invisible in that lost hour,
   Where a girl holds cut flowers and, it seems,
Suspended in a brilliant afternoon,
   The bride looks to the sky and the groom beams.
And the clock is floating like a skull-white moon.

III. VISITING COUPLE KISSING AND HALVED ONION

Unjustly I've imposed upon my friends
This? It's an onion that's been cut in half
When they're (how shall I say?) making amends
Right in the middle of the photograph,
After a night of words, and here they stand
Less like those pure, textbook transparencies
Wrapped up in one another, hand in hand,
Than layered and opaque identities,
An arm around a shoulder, face to face,
Developed in the dark to this full kit
And captured in this rapturous embrace.
Which has so many tears inside of it.

IV. Portrait of the Artist's Feet with High Top Mtn.

Now this one shows, quite accidentally,
Little Cove Gap is nestled in below
My feet, but even the casual viewer can see
Old High Top, whose great seams and ridges show
That "I am large," that I am able to stand
Above light morning haze, as I look down
On the whole picture, into the borderland,
Across the lawns and lake of Sutton Town,
Whitmanian, for "I contain multitudes"
Whose folk, today, seem to have set a fire
Under my foot that spans these latitudes!
And the smoke rises in a perfect spire.

V. Girl Hugging Snowman
with Broken Goddamn Radiator

Cute, isn't she? It's 1992.
I called him "Iron Will." In him, you see

We made a "'no'man," her allusion to
My nemesis, pure lack of sympathy,

Our gendered language, cold fact, artifice,
That chilly air. Maybe it's wrong to read this

And Wallace Stevens. If I reminisce,
Picture the way our human hearts mislead us.

It's just a snapshot out of way back when
The thing was just a radiator, right?

And we were talking, vowing to try again.
Which didn't work, especially at night.

VI. Photo Album with Visiting Couple Misfolding Afghan

> There was a story in this book, signed "Luv."
My friend, he saw it as a goof; his wife,
> She thought it cute. It'd be a record of
A Möbius strip, the "story of our life,"
> The birthdays, weddings, homes, reunions, showers,
Where every chapter's end is a fresh start,
> With space for "new adventures" we'd call "ours,"
As if life were a book, as if it's art,
> As if our real future weren't a grave
And we're the heroes, lovable, sublime,
> Misunderstanding. That book's now just another page.
In some romance that started "once upon a time."

VII. Sea Surface Full Of Crowds

                    A silly title. This isn't Tehuantepec.
It's a lawn party, and in the foreground
               It's the Yucatan coast. Seen from the upper deck,
Someone has told a joke. Observe the round
               Folds of chiffon cascade and the sea swells
Of laughter: gaping mouths, a girl's hair thrown
               Into the cold and permanent marcels
Around her neck, the man in herringbone
               Swept by the tide, while the sun's filigree
Catching the hostess's eye in this tableau
               Embellishes an opalescent sea.
Of carefree faces, taken years ago.

VIII. Portrait of the Artist's Back with Clouds

        Hey, that's me. Caught wholly unaware,
Recalling a "cloud" was once a "rock" or "hill,"
        I'm looking out the window. Standing there,
The clouds are framed and stationary. Still,
        Seeing myself in this, I'm struck to find
They turn to erratic phantoms, and they float
        Across the living room, in the back of my mind,
Like empty cartoon bubbles, though you'll note
        How little I have changed. It's the same old view
Darkening now beyond the blue moraine
        In the same old window I keep turning to.
A line of thunderstorms and sheets of rain.

IX. View of a Neighborhood in West Nashville with UFO

        ***Five years have passed . . .* But you might ask, *monjeers*,**
What's that up in the corner? It's, uh, well,
        Why I enlarged this. What you're seeing here's
A UFO. I haven't been able to tell
        My old hometown. And though I can't detect
If it's a blemish on the lens or, say,
        If I've deceived myself, I recollect
The official mess kit of the BSA,
        The sound of two-stroke engines, wreaths of smoke,
Hovering out of context, high above
        Forsythia, hot asphalt. These evoke
My former home, or else the vision of
        My former home. But nowadays I see
A spaceship. It's the sort of craft that brings
        Perplexing thoughts of what's become of me.
An alien to old familiar things.

X. Self-Portrait of the Artist in a Mirror with Ghost

Between calm self-reflection and self-love
I have exposed an apparition that
        Is a fine line. Here is an image of
(Diminishing) returns. We're looking at
        Artist qua artist. (But the dope's disguised
A distant boy, who shows up like a ghost
        By his own devices.) Oh, I've glamorized
From time to time, but I see a goal post,
        Myself, and add, not stressing it unduly,
A ball. And I've discerned, by looking hard,
    My friends, old flames, why, you can see right through me.
A boy shooting a ball in the backyard.

XI. Girl on Bicycle with American Kestrel

> **I didn't notice until I got the prints**
The sideburns unmistakably demark
> **The man, high in the picture, on a fence,**
A kestrel, a.k.a. a sparrow hawk,
> **A shy and unobtrusive citizen,**
Perched in the playground just outside of town,
> **Watching the neighbor girl on her new Schwinn,**
Head tilted slightly sideways, looking down
> **In her enormous helmet, fighting tears,**
Where, following the line of sight, it looks
> **Because her cuff is hung up in the gears.**
Like a limp goldfinch dangling from sharp hooks.

XII. Holiday Mall
with LONG FENCE

This is the mall at Christmastime. Outside,
This is a schoolyard fence. It's a LONG FENCE.
The minivans have rolled in like a tide.
Notebook paper is blown against the fence.
Lampposts are hung with cherubs and big hearts
Where vines of razor wire coil, with steel shivs,
Over the Bradford pears and shopping carts.
There is the Maytag box where someone lives.
There's Claus. There is Madonna's name in lights.
A wet skunk scrapes a soup can with his fist.
There go the young and old suburbanites.
The fence beads in a fine, acidic mist.

XIII. Appalachian Trees Encircled by Police Tape

       Conveying the effects of atmosphere,
Yellow police tape bounds a tranquil place.
       It's my *plein air* Impressionist landscape. Here
It's a crime scene, another open case.
       The trees are being poisoned, dying, like Swift,
But the authorities refuse to talk
       From the top down. Wordsworthian breezes drift
About it all. An outline's drawn in chalk;
       From heartland and high hills to the town square,
They're checking for prints. We know the scene by heart,
       But something's in the air, in the plain air.
(Where inspiration's said to come for art).

XIV. Medical School Skeleton with Dominoes Pizza Man

Superbowl XXX. And see, strung-out and thin,
The skeleton has been exposed against
The Dominoes Pizza man, enveloped in
A black felt background. Poor Bones, he's been flensed.
That baggy uniform, a backwards cap,
He's pierced; he's heroin chic; but he's all grins,
Come from the darkness in his rattletrap,
Burlesquer, rake, this rack of candlepins,
Giving long odds, right here at the front door,
A real smoothie, with a faint ennui,
And winning the bet he'll be returning for.
Another working stiff, like you or me.

               (Or was it XXXI? Oh well.) That's Anne.
And look who's back in this one: portrait style,
           You see, Anne's dancing with the pizza man,
Our old friend Bonesy, with the killer smile,
              Doing a sort of earthy, homegrown bop,
With those dark, bedroom eyes and the cleft chin,
                Belting it out like soul with ZZ Top,
But think about his humble origin,
            Buoyant with life, *jouissance*, the growing buzz
About tough prizes won along the way
                And toasted. But, then, everybody was.
Becoming much the man you see today.

Illusionist? No, friends. And nor am I
Ladies and gentlemen, The Great Bob, not
A mere man. I, bard, shall transmogrify
His real name, shall turn a plain silk knot
By the pure power of voice, by words alone,
To mourning doves. The crowd has doubts, and so
To ethereal music crows. Thus, I intone,
Do I. Rabbits crawl out of a hat. Gowns flow.
"Sincerity, strong feelings, turn to song!"
Bob waits. No magic? Has the spell gone flat?
Time passes. Nothing? I wonder what went wrong.
I said these things myself. It can't be that.

XVII. The Fifth Race at Pimlico with Pommel Horse

The jockeys drive their horses, sinewy sleek,
From cobwebbed windows, light yellows, from dust and wax,
Right through the line. The colts blur as they streak
By the bleachers, where brass names darken on plaques
Beside still banners. They're all in this pho-
To passing champions, and here, of course,
To finish. Notice, however (wouldn't you know?),
A guy in a sweatshirt works the pommel horse,
My horse, out of the running, lapped way back,
But you can't tell if he's been thrown from there,
Dead last, a mudder on today's fast track.
To heartfelt sighs, or if it's the Thomas Flair.

XVIII. D.C. in Rain
with Something Out of Focus

        Oh, come now. *Really*. Oh, but I mean *really*.
Really, now. Really but I do *mean*.

        It's, *pardon moi* the vulgar, "touchy-feely."
The pinkish blue swabs whiffling in between

        These street scenes are just *so* pedestrian.
The fogs of green are *ter*ribly embarrassing.

        (One *so* tires of clichés, now, doesn't one?)
Art must needs something more. *Really;* I mean,

        Brick fronts, neon; the cart in the turn lane!
These abstract forms! Surely they don't suggest

        A *window* box? Oh! And in slashing rain.
Mere pools of rose say more than we could have guessed.

XIX. Plumber in Crawl Space
under New York City Skyline

> **Oh, look, the City. That famous silhouette,**
You're seeing through the kitchen floor. We're doing
> **New York! Just think, Chrysler, the Yankees, the Met,**
All the plumbing. Since we knocked off gluing
> **Off-Broadway, Chelsea, Soho, the hot spots**
For lunch, we're sweating with the solder and flux
> **Of all those lives, G.E., Trump, Crown, and lots**
And lots of copper pipe. "Gravity sucks,"
> **You might say of Pop Art. I ♥ NY,**
Says the T-shirt. That's me there underneath
> **MOMA, the Frick, the 92nd St. Y.**
With a blowtorch, and a pencil in my teeth.

          There's nothing in the frame. What's *that* portray?
A perfect shot? The blank expression, square,
          A metafiction, fraud, the frame *per se*,
Pure stance, where he in fact caught only air,
          An artlessness? It's how you look at it,
And our two stoned friends shake with laughter just
          Outside the frame. Opinion tends to split:
As sweatered purists walk by with disgust.
          Believing it's a gimmick, just a ruse,
They shake their heads at all these antics. Yup,
          The moral critics want to see some *views*.
Their disapproval always cracks me up.

        Overexposed. It's just a plain white square.
In chemical emulsion, on a white sheet,
        It isn't steam or snow. But one's aware
I have produced pure art and the defeat
        Of its relation to the breath-fogged lens
Of representational nature. It's the end
        Of windows, winter skies, the socked-in fens
Of mediated feeling, and the end
        Of the Old World, the drapes, scarves, shrouds, and all
Of shopworn art. We can decertify
        Those classical illusions which enthrall.
The nineteenth-century, Romantic "I".

XXII. Billboard with
Woman in a Mirror

Words fail, as poets have always known. That's scripture.
Looks are deceiving. This is no exception.
 The sign boasts, IT'S A GOOD SIGN. GET THE PICTURE?
Not only is the "subject" a reflection,
 As you can see, I got it. The print's set,
But really it's the diva, Paul, in drag,
 In white, beside a smushed-out cigarette,
And *he* said, "Girl, '*ceci n'est pas une*' fag."
 As if the *signi*—— Aw, you know the cant.
It all seems plain, then, pow, the switcheroo.
 Look, don't just take my word for it. You can't.
Believe me. Everything I say is true.

XXIII. RECLINING NUDE WITH WILDFLOWERS SIGN I

        Studio work. I don't much care for it.
I like the open road. Off to one side
      Here's my compulsory nude. You've got to admit,
The WILDFLOWERS sign has double-crossed us, lied;
        However, she's a fox. In the wide bed
There are no flowers. Still, it brings to mind
     She strikes a conventional pose, arms carefully spread,
A fabricated scene that is designed
      To flaunt, seduce, exquisitely engage,
By art alone, like those Spenserian bowers,
     Seeming to come alive from the flat page.
Lush with spectacular absences of flowers.

XXIV. Reclining Nude with Wildflowers Sign II

The studio was a friend's. It's the same shot.
The sign's still there. Closer inspection shows
     I've gotten double prints. But she is not
An old association with the rose,
     Another pretty face to be consumed,
Deflowered by teenage boys or Father Time,
     Nor some air-brushed Edenic Eve who bloomed
As Beauty herself. Because of the word, I'm
     Back in a private garden. She's the friend.
Thinking of flowers, but seeing they're not there,
     I helped her do self-portraits. In the end
I'm left, more or less, with paradox, thin air:
     Nothing was ever shown. What's all this mean?
WILDFLOWERS creates, invokes, is standing as
     A world of difference, as we have seen.
A sign, "the which a double nature has."

These were my neighbors. It's a big group pose:
On mist-gray skies, the stark, black branches etch
Horizon, lawn, in loose haphazard rows.
As if in tin, or as in some old sketch,
That's The Great Bob. And that's our good Queen Paul
Whose lines, whose every nuance was precise,
With Champagne Anne and Rick the dog. They're all
But faded now. I've seen the trees in ice,
Decked out (Liz, too, who helped me do the plumbing),
But I'll be gone when their spring blooms and scatters
Even the children. And, God, they're all becoming.
Shades, as the new leaves turn to other matters.

XXVI. Half Border Collie,
Half Black Strip

Ruined. That's it. That makes the whole damn roll.
It's a sunset. In warm, declining light,
        I tried for an extra print; got a black hole:
The dog is leaping for, poised in midflight,
        An emblematic darkness swallowing
A Frisbee. There he stays, suspended in
        The present tense, where night keeps following
A setting sun, as if he's always been
        The final frame. Tomorrow, I pretend,
In hot pursuit, graceful as one can be,
        I'll start anew. Today, I've come to the end.
Chasing after something I can't see.

III.

New Year's:
A Short Pantoum

The sunlight was falling. A part
Played out in the deep snow.
We were all there. At the start
We knew how the year would go,

Played out in the deep snow.
The sunlight was falling apart.
We knew how the year would go.
We were all there at the start.

And Another Thing
about the Leaves

They've come unglued. They're shaken in their quires
And like Empedocles on Etna fling
Themselves despairing down into backyard fires
(Which, by the way, have been illegalized),
Leaving behind the worn, bare, ruined choirs
Of winter, leaving, that is, the scaffolding:
These late leaves have routinely symbolized

In many celebrated verses (A)
Sere, jaundiced, hoary-headed old age; (B)
The toe-tagged multitudes, the DOA,
Afoot in purely rhetorical shades; and (C)
Our print-text medium itself, the *a*
Priori burthen of all those ISB
Ns, dating several centuries BC.

The hearts and limbs are plunged in the deep freeze,
These hardened arteries, these wiring schemes,
These tapered, finial ends of family trees
All at a height, like a mass extinction. Here
Are the charts and fruits of genealogies—
Those branching variations on the first themes—
And solid proof of the lateness of the year.

The naked truth, right here in black and white,
Chilly, unlovely, stark.

We'd wish, instead,
Another spring, a wash of honeyed light,
A cover band of warblers, doing the hits,
Clean scents of chive and jasmine, the all-night
Gymnastic horseplay of the dorm-room bed,
The ornamentals' fragile, stage-show glitz,

And wish, could we go back, a green expanse
Of fresh-faced leaves, of lofty aspirations,
Veiling the scaffold in the latest dance,
Blithely aloof to their own DNA
Where is encrypted the boggling role of chance,
The timed assaults, creative adaptations,
And the notarized termination of their stay.

Three-Sided,
One-Way Mirror

From the collage of arts and sciences,
       Those two old houses, I,
Last in my line, indebted, classify
       In twin respects as "glass."
If I'm all sil——, all *argentine* panache,
       Glinting along each spine,
Some Merlin's slick mirage, some monkeyshine,
       In which is briskly spun
The multifaceted faces Anyone
       Puts on, time and again,
In the flattering and high-tech halogen
       Refulgence of the mall,
Interrelatedly representational
       As all the vertiginous play
Of, say, semantics, that's one view, one way
       Of looking at it, true.

But look again. You see? You see right through.
       Biomechanically
A dark view. Out there in those shadowy
       Lands of the latest fad,
Ensembles come and go, the ironed-clad,
       The pressed, the skirted. I
Watch coats of arms (if art should edify)
       Like vestments of the dead,
The limbless dummies, pinned, straight-jacketed,
       Chiffons stretched on the rack,

Heads on a pike, the blood-red, cardiac-
     Thatched G-strings, belts that are
All suitable for hanging, . . . a bazaar
     Of horrors. As they say,
Best never to be born.

          Now one fine day,
     Who should come flashing on
My sil——, my *argentine* Palladian
     But H___. Her eyen gray,
Her several lovely persons ricochet
     Throughout my bailiwick.
And, ah, they're all in love, all hurt, heartsick.
     And right on cue, expert,
A young man in a Red Cross donor's shirt
     Sidles across my row.
H___ goes off humming, *pianissimo.*
     I'm going to miss all this.
(Forgive an old mirror that would reminisce.)
     I'm being replaced by *them*,
For which I've no device, no stratagem,
     Those literal, one-eyed, flat-
File cameras.
          And in my habitat
     Lights dim. Doors close. It's drab.
My dark side darkens gravely. Shadows gab.
     I re-envision my mad,
Ongoing project, my *Scintilliad*,
     Collecting, if you will,
In what I call a retrospectacle,
     Back glances, indirections,
Sparks of insight gleaned from long reflections
     On myself, swan song
Of the silver fog . . . ; and should I bear a strong
     Resemblance—debonair,

Polished, inheriting a certain flair—
      To the main character,
Composing, as something of a pasticheur,
      His own *Chanson de Glass*
Whose razzmatazz's surface's pizzazz
      Turns trope, I think of *his*
Main character, poised on the sore abyss,
      Compiling impressions for
L'Image du Mall, whose modern troubadour,
      Late come, diminished, too
Aware, suffers continual déjà vu
      And, strictly *démodé*,
Reflects upon his own internal play
      And point of no return,
His vanishing act in our patrolling, stern
      Back room, long home of the soul,
And is, as well (past his or my control),
      A limpid, lidless eye
Placed *here* to take it all in, to stand by
      (While friends on the cleaning crew
Get one more day prepared for me and you
      In full, life-size 3-D)
And stare out at *our place* in history.

The Muse
Addresses the Poet
(and getteth alle up
in hys face)

Just where do you get off, pal? Whoop-de-doo,
You found out words are fickle, that they lie
Right to your face. You boob, of course they do.
The first thing language did was ramify
Into a wandering wood as old as I
Am. Spenser scooped you. What's more, in a word
My good friend Harry Bailey might supply,
"Thy drasty rhyming is nat worth a toord."

Where'd I go wrong? Why do you still imbue
Creeks, flowers, leaves, moons, clouds, the whole
       dang sky
With hints of you? Even the old scops knew
That's unbacked specie, scrip that couldn't buy
The paper it's printed on, and as you tie
Some arbitrary value to a bird,
I'm not sure how to put this, but I'll try,
"Thy drasty rhyming is nat worth a toord."

Where was I? Oh, right. Lookit here, we're through
If you don't ditch that cluck you glorify,
Who's bored us all for aeons with his mew,
His pangs and inconveniences, the high
Regard for what he calls "My Self" (my eye!),

That tedious biography . . . ! I've heard
All I can stomach of him, and by the by,
"Thy drasty rhyming is nat worth a toord."

The self-love. The sin*cer*ity! The sigh.
I've heard it all before. You're such a nerd.
Now tell your book to git. *Envoi.* Goodbye.
"Thy drasty rhyming is nat worth a toord."

"The Mockingbird
Is Imitating Life"

You've probably read up on birds, by which
I don't mean stories where a nightingale
or thrush or whatnot turns up out of nowhere—
nature, I guess, or anyway somewhere else
outside us—in a time of personal
despair. That's pretty much irrelevant
these days: We've moved on, and around these parts
the trees and grass, as someone put it once,
have been expunged and razed. I'm talking facts.
The mockingbird, or *Mimus polyglottos*,
famed as a "rapturous singer on moonlit nights
among magnolias" is, of course, a "fine,
fine mimic." He can sound like anything.
    Well, as it was, I'd gone down to the store.
It was December, cold and drizzly. Phone
lines, full of solicitations, scored the sky.
Streetlights were coming on, and in the mist
they looked like nimbuses, or what I thought
the ignis fatuus might look like. This
was the atmosphere of graveyards. Vapors and fogs
rose out of storm grates and incinerators,
swirled in brake lights, rose as exhalations
from two men flipping each other off, from me,
the faceless hoods of raincoats, and the woman
coming my way, who gripped her car keys like
a gimlet, as we're taught, so if the need
arises you can poke out someone's eye.

That's when I saw the mockingbird. Sour, wet,
tattered, with patches on his wings, he perched
high up on a surveillance camera
outside of Royal Farms. And there we stood:
One celebrated "territorial mimic,"
"official bird of five southeastern states,"
"musical singer of endless variation,"
and one late-twentieth-century American,
captured on video tape in a cold rain
gazing skyward from a concrete stoop.
And check this out: you know what he was doing?
That threadbare, deadpan, patched-together bird,
"habitually raising his wings archangel-wise,"
was mocking the car alarms, going like,
"Whooop, whooop, whooop, whooop, whooop."

December 31, 2000

?
.

The parrot on my shoulder begins to giggle
Into his wing. The sled dogs bite their lips.
Orange is the sky at night, and orange
My face and hands. Tall
Is my terrible feather. How long
We've been seeking X, to find the sound
We thought was wind in the harp of a tree
Was piped in through the ductwork and X,
O elusive apostrophized X, is some
Nonlinear $f(X)$ in a feedback loop.
My figurehead blows on her nails. All
But washed up, the moon, with its golf balls
And go-carts, gives a big stage wink
To the fourth wall. And tall is my terrible feather.

Someday, my quests for a journey done, the moon
Retired, I'll download what was once "the night sky,"
Long since turned tale, turned into folklore,
And tell the children gathered around my knee about
The constellation known to some as the Big Sickle,
To others, Signum Quaestionis, the Question Mark,
That cast of stars by which the old,
Old ones, Sir Ceaseless, Lady Brokenheart,
Wandered their wander. And the children
Will laugh at my beard and misdoubt the very screen
And coo over my antique and loquacious parrot,
Who was in on the joke from the start.

[from] In Search of
The Forgotten Woman[1]

10W-40, go to pay
And meet a stranger in the checkout lines
Who in a foreign accent points the way,
"Go W. 4 mi., turn L., and watch for signs."
My Pacer,[2] with its poor acceleration,
Makes free of the station.

(Here endeth Book VI)

BOOK VII

The Poet-   If truth is beauty, beauty
Quester   Must be as trendy and provisional
goeth to a   As truth, in true life down the thoroughfare
fantastical   Just off I-95 to Springfield Mall
land   In Alexandria, Virginia, where
    The field and spring were paved, square-
        footage sold,
    And fully automated rheostats
    Adjust the lighting in a cool, controlled
    Environment for all of us mall rats
    Under discreet surveillance by off-duty

---

[1]Book VII and the few lines that conclude Book VI and begin Book VIII are the only extant fragments of this Romantic Epic. The title suggested by previous editors has been adopted here. The marginal notes are presumed to have been supplied during a later transcription.

[2]"Pacer" is probably an intentional archaism, since the appellation was obsolete by the date of composition. Convention often posits the horse as symbolic of poetic vehicle, but that is unlikely here. Cf. the equally literal horses of Robert Browning's "Childe Roland to the Dark Tower Came" and James Wright's "In Memory of the Horse David, Who Ate One of My Poems."

2.

Undercover cops and video
Camcorders which transmit
Digitized pictures to Security.
Along the corridor, I search the row
in search of Of Glamour Shots,[3] Gold Standard, Odyssey
a legendary For The Forgotten Woman, then traverse
woman.[4] A cantilevered mezzanine, which bends
Past ficus trees, Another Universe,
Occasions Hallmark, Things Remembered,
       Trends,
And dead-ends at Petite Sophisticate.

3.

He's lost. I'm lost. But lost, I see, among confreres.
There's Mae and Harry, in a ProServe cap—
Two senior citizens
With Sony Walkmans, wristbands,[5] Nike Airs,
He meeteth And dichromatic warm-ups from the Gap.
companions. Behind them three anemic truants lean
And loaf with nose rings,[6] sagging
       corduroys,
And geometric haircuts out of *Teen.*
In front there's Buster with Transformer
       toys,
His mom, and green balloons from Bennigan's.

---

[3]"Glamour Shots . . . Petite Sophisticate": Tradition has seen the place-names as outrageous inventions, therefore as allegorical topoi of false or debased art. Contemporary scholarship has verified the names, however, and reads them without irony.

[4]Marginal commentary has been taken to imply the object of the quest is the tripartite Goddess-Muse-Maiden, a mythopoeic symbol of artistic inspiration. This is in error.

[5]"wristbands": wide, elasticized strips of terry cloth, worn as ornamentation.

[6]"nose rings": Then, as now, nose rings had totemic significance, esp. as worn by virgins of the harvest cults. (Hence the phrase, "ring out, the old; ring in, the new.")

4.

They are
spellbound
by a
vision

They're standing very still. Behind the show-
Room window is a striking mannequin.
One leg is angled to a pointed toe.
Her head is cocked. Her small
Hand seems to grasp a sudden thought. She's
        in
A double-breasted houndstooth business
        suit,
Notched collar plunging to a daring V,
A matching, A–line miniskirt, and cute
Black T–strap pumps. We're wondering if she
Is really fake or else a living doll.

5.

and begin
to quarrel
over her
magical
arts.

The pitch is "New Look for a Classic."[7] Mae,
However, and I'm paraphrasing, thinks,
"A businesswoman wouldn't dress that way:
The neckline's frivolous; the pattern stinks;
And clients wouldn't trust her."
Harry is troubled by her attitude:
"She's awkward, mannered, definitely fake."
One of the truants answers, "No way, dude."
There's silence after that. Then Buster gives
        his take,
"She's pretty, Mom." And I agree with
        Buster.

[7]"Classic": Contemporary scholarship disputes this term.

6.

Brown eyes, the recessed lighting on her
        cheek,
She wears an Apple Frost lip liner, blush,
And Winter Sky mascara from Clinique.
Her office is a vinyl desk, a plush
Red blotter, and a cardboard phone from Bell,
A super- A scene which Harry adds
natural Is "too contrived." And all the while, we're
sentience cased
watches By some bored sentry in a secret cell,[8]
from beyond. Observing us, the pane, and her wasp waist,
Accentuated by her shoulder pads.

7.[9]

A perfect figure. She's a cynosure,
This artful, working model of perfection,
As we stand here objectifying her.
Then, with a little smirk in our direction,
She straightens, flips her hair behind an ear,

[8]Again, marginal commentary is in error to suggest an allegorical significance to
the superior presence that observes the narrative proceedings from an external van-
tage. Archaeological investigation has produced compelling evidence that "mall" coun-
try was, in fact, heavily patrolled by deputies of the state.
    [9]This inferior stanza was discovered in a discarded ms., presumably earlier:
            A perfect figure. On a pedestal,
            Behind glass, she's a life-sized imitation
            Of true . . . [the manuscript's illegible
            Through here] . . . and with a look of irritation
            Turns on the platform, steps down, and departs.
            She *is* alive! a businesswoman, real,
            Who's made up as a doll
            Who's made up as a woman who by arts
            Is made up in an industry ideal
            Of beauty that's entirely natural.

Turns on the platform,[10] steps down, and
        departs

The dispute   Into a life beyond
continues   My looking, nodding to the young cashier,
about the   Her disappearing waistline pinned in darts.
truth of   Mae says, "I'll bet she's not a real blonde."
the vision.

8.

Show's over. Mom lifts Buster. Harry clears
The lap time on his watch. The truants hike
Their pants. And in the window[11] there
        appears
A point-by-point transparent lookalike
In Converse high tops, T–shirt from J. Crew,
He seeth   And jeans by Levi Strauss, in whom I see
a phantom A limited first-person point of view,
in the   Verisimilitude
medium.   Of the true self, a spitting image: me.
A voice across the mall says, "No way, dude."

9.

Occasions, Trends, Another Universe—
I come upon the mall's directory,
Some disappointment, and, a little worse
For where, walk past the costume jewelry
Of Silver Dolphin, Afterthoughts Boutique,
By Natural Wonders, Century 21,

[10]"platform": Some critics have suggested that this stanza alludes ironically to the long tradition of artistic creations, often on pedestals, becoming vivified. Cf. Ovid's myth of Pygmalion and Galatea in *The Metamorphoses*. These suggestions should be treated skeptically, however, since such business practices were commonplace and there are no traces of irony.

[11]"window": In a standard pane of glass, 94% of the photons from a light source pass through; 6% reflect. The identity of the "lookalike" has never been determined.

And through the wrong door out into the
        squeak
Of disc brakes and the sky-high midday sun,
A failed amanuensis,
A bar code in a demographic census.

10.

What's true? I take the northbound
        interchange

He resumeth
his quest.

In search of The Forgotten Woman. John
Deere[12] backhoes roam the clear-cut hills.
        Styles change.
The living mannequins keep moving on.
Soon Mae mall walks alone three times a
        week.
The truants pass the Bar. Down a long hall
Buster wipes his daughter's infant cheek.
But still there is the window, through it all
Impassive, cold, and only as clear as glass,
In which the true lives pass.

(*Here endeth Book VII*)[13]

---

[12]John Deere invented the first rudimentary tractor. In a note found among the ms. pages, an unknown scribe makes two perplexing citations. The first mentions an Indo-European myth in which a hunter pursues a deer deep into a forest where the deer transforms into a (perhaps supernatural) woman. In the second he quotes the line, "I am of them that furthest cometh behind," from Sir Thomas Wyatt's "Whoso List to Hunt," which he describes as a poem about "fruitless quest" and "poetic belatedness." Since this is such an obvious misreading, the notes have generally been disregarded and may be unrelated to the ms.

[13] The fragmentary lines that follow hint only at a resumption of the quest, a mysterious "White Castle," and a "traffic stop," a government-backed shakedown or ancient form of taxation.

Still Lost at Sea

Half-baked, half-drowned, at wit's end, Anyone
Would harbor doubts about the "fishy plot"
That fetched him there, the "yarn old liars spun"
Of empty strands, where now this Erronaut
Wanders a sun-bleached Isle of Sounds, Key Quest,
His Isle of Mien, where things were what they *seemed*
And he's a plain fiasco, just a geste,
A message in a bottle (and one deemed
By experts, when it finally surfaced, prank),

So that he dubbed himself Sir Title, viz.,
All Talk, or Words To That Effect, one No
One, No One who was Anyone, and sank
Nightly in ink-dark seas, immersed in his
Near-drowning, documented in the glow
Of small fires, while the high romantic moon,
That's heard it all, rose over his lagoon,
Over the whole volcanic chain, its bays
Leaf green, its islands full of castaways.

The Life and Times
of Wile E. Coyote,
Super Genius

I am a genius by trade.
W. E. COYOTE

With you afling, afang, not yet nonplussed,
Nemesis Roadrunner, Swift-footed, Taker-of-three-
Forks, strange kinetic fellow, animated
Character, that pluméd cuckoo, Bird
Thou never wert, sticks out his tongue, waves, peels
Out, and you wrap up a pileated
Bust of smoke. And now? What now? "I must
Dream up a *bril*liant master strategy,

Ing*en*ious, *dar*ing." Here's to you, Coyote.
Here's to Giant Fly Traps, Quick-Dry Cements,
To ACME Robots, glues, kites, keyhole saws,
DO-IT-YOURSELF TORNADOS, female bird
Impersonations, anvils, Earthquake Pills, . . .
And to the selective repeal of natural laws,
Schemus Backfiribus, a reverse Quixote:
Art turns to mere truth, what it represents,

Then, proven to be true, it turns fictitious.
Roadrunner goes right over the painted span,
You fall to the canyon floor, and from the phony
Tunnel comes the train, *engineered by the bird*,
Your foison, fantasy, feather in your cap,
The better life, your failure—like my own.
Wile E. Everyman. Come, Trickster, let us
Feast on our clay chicken, our tin can.

Riddles

(time limit—20 minutes)

Example:
  With a high pitch, I leave home in my flights
  Over your fields and parks. On summer nights
  I sweep the sky. Though blind, I get lost in the lights.

1.   In a dark chamber, commonly, I thrive.
      I have been shot, and yet I'm still alive.
      Though people think to hang me, I survive.

2.   From obscure stations, raised to this full height,
      I ride the waves. (A sailboat? That's not right.)
      When we have parted, I drop out of sight.

3.   No forest, still I'm full of trees, you know.
      They made me what I am. And even though
      They're planted, where I take them, there they go.

4.   I make up words, but I am no one's fool,
      Was in the top five in my class at school,
      Help write the laws, and yet I do not rule.

5.   I worked in a cramped style to be quite frank,
      And grew more weary as the numbers shrank.
      Bird is to me, as pale moon is to _____.

6.   Rapacious, I grow fat, but not content.
      I swell, go forth and multiply; augment.
      I stick it to you, come and leave you spent.

7.   I've got no ax or knife, don't pull or smother,
        And yet when I assert myself, oh brother,
        I separate one party from another.

8.   I dwell on you; to me your eyes are shut.
        I follow you, but blithely on you strut.
        Just what do you take me for, . . . ?

9.   I go on your head, but neither hat nor hair,
        Nor hood nor wig nor wreath, yet yours to wear.
        So live a little, friend. I'll meet you there.

10.   Based in good measure on an old design,
        I'm, oh, about yea long. With me and mine,
        Step by step, you come to the end of the line.

11.   Dismissed as irresponsible, it's true
        I kid, dissemble, feign, and misconstrue.
        Why the long face? That's just between me and you.

12.   Speaking in code, I mean more than I say.
        Much is between the lines (so what's new, eh?),
        Behind the palisades of self-display.

Answer Sheet

Example: A. Bat
             B. Ball
             C. Libra
             D. A and E
             E. C and D

1.   ☐ A. Rifle
      ☐ B. Photograph
      ☐ C. Moon
      ☐ D. The foundling, Tom Jones
      ☐ E. Dice

2.   ☐ A. Crest
      ☐ B. Human body
      ☐ C. Pop star
      ☐ D. Hand
      ☐ E. Comb

3.   ☐ A. Acorn
      ☐ B. Sailing ship
      ☐ C. *The Audubon Society Field Guide to North American Trees*
      ☐ D. Person
      ☐ E. Termite

4.   ☐ A. C
      ☐ B. E
      ☐ C. A
      ☐ D. B
      ☐ E. D

5. ☐ A. Flock, night sky
    ☐ B. Nest, fingernail
    ☐ C. Finger, buttocks
    ☐ D. Thomas Hardy, William Butler Yeats
    ☐ E. Dodo, blank

6. ☐ A. HMO industry
    ☐ B. Locusts
    ☐ C. Ponzi scheme
    ☐ D. Association of Trial Lawyers of America
    ☐ E. E. coli

7. ☐ A. Political platform
    ☐ B. Comma
    ☐ C. Centrifuge
    ☐ D. Divorce court
    ☐ E. Hangover

8. ☐ A. A doting mutt
    ☐ B. An idiot
    ☐ C. The scuttlebutt
    ☐ D. Some kind of nut
    ☐ E. Your own personal butt

9. ☐ A. Lump
    ☐ B. Tombstone
    ☐ C. Blame
    ☐ D. Lampshade
    ☐ E. Price

10. ☐ A. Foot
    ☐ B. Foot
    ☐ C. Foot
    ☐ D. Foot
    ☐ E. Both A and C

11.   □   A. Riddle
      □   B. Poet
      □   C. Joke
      □   D. Paronomasia
      □   E. Fable

12.   □   A. All of the above
      □   B. Tattoo
      □   C. Personal ad
      □   D. Bar code
      □   E. Vanity tag

Binocular Diplopia

I've tried, Lord knows,
To keep from seeing double. . . .
JAMES MERRILL

Life was a blur. Or so he thought. The thing
Was, he'd been diagnosed with a small-time
Astigmatism. Why think otherwise?
But when the doctor told him, "Read the chart,"
And he replied, "Which one?" even the smart
Young nurse said, "Uh oh." As for him, his eyes
Were opened and he saw, for the first time,
That he was seeing two of everything.

This would explain a lot. In stereoscopic
Hindsight he reviewed old patterns of
Mistakes: missed shots, a lifetime of misreading,
Mixed signals (this as the nurse was double-knitting
Her cute brows), false moves, smashed thumbs from
      hitting
The wrong nail on the head, all finally leading
To how the woman he first fell in love
With turned to myth. But that's another topic.

Meanwhile, the long walk home. Or rather two.
A second one appeared to levitate,
Illusive, epiphanic, and oblique—
Like dual reflections in a double pane
Of glass, or some self-referential strain
Of allegory. Which one, so to speak,

Was true? If seeing's believing, not the great
Sam Johnson could refute it: Both were true.

Twinned like a postcard's double-stamped cachet,
The phone lines added up to musical staves,
With a score of birds; Shell's logo seemed to shine
Like a big con; and everywhere he turned,
His second nature brazenly returned
Equivocations in the plainest sign,
From the pecuniary, JESUS SAVES
To the unwittingly blunt SLOW CHILDREN AT PLAY,

As if the world were, after all, a text,
"A book in folio," a hieroglyph.
Here was the uncorrected proof. The elder's
Two thick volumes of belated leaves
And, spiraling in double helices,
Its legendary keys all seemed to tell,
Beside themselves, another tale, as if
These traces were the cryptic analects

Of some long-lost original. (Or flim-
flam! Now get real. This is pure grandstanding.
Look in thy heart, etc.) Double trouble.
Even close introspection was abased.
With two left feet, twin-featured and two-faced,
He saw, head down, foreshortened in a puddle,
Under a critical sign that said, NO STANDING,
Me. (When was it I turned into him?)

So that was that. And he (we'll say) set out
Again, flung open the double doors to find
Her smiling faces, whom he'd fancied for
So long as muse, and girl back home, and quest,
And so much more. Closing his eyes to rest
He saw her image turn from metaphor
To perfect vision, singular, clear, defined,
The one thing he had always dreamt about.

Errors in the Script

1.

Just as the roller makes its final pass,
Plows under the last uncultivated swath
Of "Dandelion Green" down in the last
Corner of the last room, sprinkling drop cloth
And me with a cool mist in the evening's shade,
We get a call. It's Corporate HQ.
My wife, paint-flecked, bandana-ed, in a braid,
Comes back struck numb: "Guess who's been
        transferred." "Who?"

We stand there side by side, my fell exten-
sion roller center foreground in the notch
Between our shoulders, like the farmers in
Grant Wood's *American Gothic*. At two paces
We and the basement, in a showdown, watch
The paint dry on each other's neutral faces.

2.

"Take care of the cat," she says. (We have a cat?)
And thus our story's savvy heroine
Saddles her Bronco, throwing a hand out in
A right-turn signal, her (in nine more easy
Payments) "champagne brown" engagement ring
Facetiously aglint. And cue the laugh—

I mean, the *sound*track, as I raise my hand
Like the new sheriff and in slow-mo half-
Surrender to a spring premiere apart,
The candlelit dissolves, her Sweeps-week fling,
My grimaced, Oscar style soliloquies,
And our faith in the formulas of art
That some stayed-tuned-for future episode
Would bring us back together down the road.

3.

My kingdom. Instantly the ficus leaves
Prostrate themselves to me. The lilies bow.
I stroll my grounds. I gaze. I wow the whole
Room with my speedwork on remote control.
(I'm totally self-taught.) And nobly now
To the round table, Our bight, to launch the long
Adventure, Our romantic quest, Our *song*,
Where ship is soul and wind in the billowing sleeves,
In the filling sheets, is pure afflatus, rife
With legends of the heart, Sir Errant, and
Like Crispin sing the genius of the C . . .

No, that must wait. The ship sinks by the quay.
Bills need my signature. I'm on dry land,
Grounded in someone's (what's this?) someone's *life*.

4.

With this ridiculous mouse that's brought to view
Mountains of pixels, e-pistles, real-time quotes
(Like Berra on DiMaggio: "He was
The greatest living player I ever saw"),

I log on Gateway ("Home"), my "portal to
The future," to download our "dream house" from
The World Wide Web @ REALTOR.COM.

Dream house? [OE. cloud castle? sugar shack?
Stanzaic rooms (too numerous to cite),
+ great lines, must-see plot.] Why, there you go,
A life in art! The dream house is the po——!
But, like this link, futures are asymptotes.
The hard drive sputters: ERROR IN SCRIPT. THIS
      SITE
IS UNAVAILABLE. The screen goes black.

5.

I call up Gateway on the telephone.
"Your call's important. For brochure, press one.
If your computer isn't booting up,
Press two. For trouble with your modem . . ." on
And on, menus galore! For hours I try
The catacombs, which lead their phone-treed pawn
To trapdoors always back to start: "Your call's . . ."

This Byzantine perfection! Goldberg maze!
Closed loops uncrackable as Bucky Balls!
I've wormholed back to Earth from Cyberspace:

There *is* no Operator standing by,
No fern-filled golden Help Room, no Web Master,

And no way out, till you, in a futile gesture,
Returning to the cradle, hang it up.

6.

The Realistic™ tuner seeks a clear
Signal: "'. . . and goeth *not* from house to house,'
He *did* say . . ." seekseekseek "An accident
Can happen when you least expect it. Here

At Graft & . . ." seekseek "We've got Tim from Trent
On BookTalk. Tim?" "Hi. Yeah. The character's
Not likable. He doesn't grow." Sue: "Worse,
The female vanished." Tim: "The dialogue

Is wooden. *Woo-dun.*" Sue: "Where's Insight?" Tim:
"Where's Dame Epiphany?" Sue: "Then we bog
Down in that call-in show. Like, who's read *him*?"
(Laughter) Tim: "Not to beat up a dead horse,

It's all so artificial, so, doggone it,
Retro for its use of . . . ,"
                              I know, words.

7. Voice-Activated Tape Recorder:

                              Note
To self: Find cat. Also, take steps to grow.

Day One of my explorations: Missed the boat.
Beginning to hear voices. Spirits low.

I've come to suspect, too late, I was beguiled
By legend, by the old words one could rely
On once, perhaps, before the theorists,
Like Geoffrey Chaucer. Voices

                                    now emphatic
About words' artifice. But we
                            held on,

Held
        to our superstitions, no?: the vatic
Text, mimesis, self, plainspokenness.
Which takes me to boyhood, something of Oscar Wilde,

That "superstition, like belief, must die,
And what remains when disbelief is gone?"

8.

Bring up the moon.
                            A shadow like a scythe,
A raptor, sweeps through the stanzas of the house,
Across the painted backdrop.
                                    Lights! And curtains.
The room goes black.
                            . . . and *goeth*. Seekseekseek.
Where's Insight? Where's
                            our Gateway? For brochure,
Press one, Sugar. Our long
                            adventure Lithe
In art The old words playing cat and mouse
Mixed up the formula.
                            What can I say?

Errors in the script accumulate
Genetically, and it's so late. But wait,

But, briefly, look! One glimpse of a distant bind:
The pilgrim, lost, checking the legend to find

Himself at the state line, turning the leaf
For a new life, still half a day away.

Errata

1. While the Foundling, Tom Jones, is accosted at gunpoint, he is not, in fact, as it turns out, shot. Protestations to the effect that "he's, he's, he's shot on *film*" in the movie starring Albert Finney have not met support in the court of public opinion. The author (should such a creature exist) regrets this misunderstanding.

2. The heading of this page, as was made evident to the author (whatever) by Douglas R. Hofstadter, should read, "Erratum."